Things of Little

Consequence

Things of Little Consequence

John Casey

PHiR Publishing
San Antonio

PHiR Publishing
San Antonio, TX
phirpublishing.com

ISBN: 979-8-9867452-8-2
Library of Congress Control Number: 2023912765

Printed in the United States of America

Also by John Casey

RAW THOUGHTS

A Mindful Fusion of Poetic and Photographic Art

(with photographer Scott Hussey)

MERIDIAN

A Raw Thoughts Book

(with photographer Scott Hussey)

DEVOLUTION

Book One of The Devolution Trilogy

EVOLUTION

Book Two of The Devolution Trilogy

REVELATION

Book Three of The Devolution Trilogy

THE BARN

A Novella Mystery

(co-authored by Doug Campbell)

"Sometimes the questions are complicated, and the answers are simple." —Dr. Seuss

Foreword

I was told it may only have worth
when it is written in a very circumlocutory manner.
Or enveloped in obscurity.

Or laced with impossibly complex analogies,
and with words that don't belong
together together.

Singularly weird and nearly incomprehensible
are what appear to make it most valuable,
to them.

Better to describe love as
"adventitious candy corn"
than ethereal sunshine.

Better to say someone in despair is
"an obfuscated polecat"
than a wintered soul.

Obfuscated polecat—

now that baby right there

might just win you some kinda golden trophy…

I was told, in fact, it is best not to attempt to philosophize

about love or loss, about challenge or struggle.

As if the elements of existence are beyond grasp for most.

…Unless, of course, you are prepared to twist them

in such alluringly demiurgic fashion

that there is barely a spider-silk thread of a connection left

between your conclusion

&

the original thought.

However,

they are not necessarily looking for

what I am looking for.

Many develop an aversion to the beauty of plain logic,

lost in a zealous quest for overly esoteric truisms

and seemingly sophisticated philosophies.

It somehow becomes easier to adhere

to the mystical, to the cryptic and the Kafkaesque

when confronted with a thousand disparate pieces of life

because we sense it would be impossible to comprehend

the grand sum of it all or how those pieces even interconnect.

Consequently, we cannot understand the individual parts.

The truth is, we can.

Life is much simpler than most believe.

Things are not so confusing as they seem.

This Moment Is All There Is

Genesis

A picture
may be worth
a thousand words,

but just a few
of the right words
can paint a thousand pictures.

Carpe Diem

Live it Learn it Work it Earn it

Climb It Run it Yell it Fun it

Like it Date it Joy it Fate it

How it Why it Hold it Cry it

Love it Leave it Miss it Grieve it

Hurt it Need it Shame it Feed it

Lie it Fake it Lose it Break it

Drug it Thrill it Hate it Kill it

Quam Minimum Credula Postero?

Pas de Deux

Her name eludes me, for now.
But it is a lesser thing.

I have instead her voice,
her stories and dreams—
words of worldly ambition and sublime imagery.
Enigmatic, arresting impressions,
toujours à la mode.

This, from a willowy, graceful siren
continually twirling,
whirling here and then there,
el corredor with the wind.
I await the next dance.

Presence

Quiet the mind.

Observe the moment.

This is possible,

even in the most distracting environments.

It is then that your more persistent worries

will lessen and disperse,

like morning mist

in a rising summer sun.

Twenty Twenty-One

In the New Year
I will remember,

on occasion,
to see you smile

from January
through December

made twenty twenty
all worthwhile.

Day Two

It was supposed to be freezing.

I brought winter clothes for us both.

Coats, gloves, a long cashmere scarf.

But we did not need them.

The air, despite the elevation,

was chock full of oxygen.

Clean, crisp, and cool, but not cold.

We could not have prayed for a more beautiful day.

It was supposed to be awkward.

The day before,

I waited at a small table near the park,

just outside La Boulangerie.

You walked up

wearing an overly large

sky blue and white checkerboard pullover.

You smiled and said *hi*...

From then, we went place to place,

moment by moment,

smile by smile

until there in the car,

with you hanging dangerously far

out the window, laughing

and taking pictures as you took it all in

while I just drove us along.

Again

in your blue checkered sweater

because it was cool,

but not cold.

I felt swindled

for being forced to keep my eyes

on the road ahead

instead of you.

We moved along and under

trees so tall you cannot see their tops.

Imposing, craggy mountains, sheer cliffs and

bridal veil waterfalls.

I wondered

with increasing anticipation,

as I stole adrenalized glimpses of you

in-between curves and other cars,

what else might lie ahead?

Because it was supposed to be many things

and as it was, it had been none of those.

And this was only day two.

Event Horizon

The past is apparition.

The future, a shifting illusion.

Time is a trick.

This moment is all there is.

Nothing Hurts Me Now

Wish

There is no requital
for the revenant reverie

of a thing
we can never have.

The Unraveling

He said he would leave her alone,
though he struggles with it.
He needs her to know he experienced an awakening.
Nothing that fixes anything, but a revelation, nonetheless.

He is at peace.
Before, he accepted it. But not without anxiety and pain.
Now he realizes there was nothing he could have done
to change her mind, or to prevent the unraveling.

He is not perfect,
but he did nothing wrong.
He now senses it was all so simply…
certain.

Together, they were fast, real, beautiful, and rare.
Fear of losing something so sublime can be overpowerful
when a strong foundation of trust, support,
and shared understanding has not yet matured.

He thinks back to the day he went to her, worried.

She did not want to see him, but relented.

Head hung low, cross-legged on the floor, she sat,

distraught and weeping.

She looked up, lamenting she did not want to lose him.

He thought, *in what world can you believe that is remotely possible?*

And he responded tenderly,

you could only ever lose me if you leave me.

But he was wrong—his thinking was off.

By leaving him,

she would never have to experience being left.

The things he wishes he said to her instead...

With time, he hopes she comes to see things as he does.

His heart is still hers, if she somehow decides to have it back.

Blank slate, reset, no expectations, unconditionally.

All he ever gave her was unconditional; his love, most of all.

Poetic Justice

Is it understandable, or is it pitiable
to be surprised
by the hollow realization
I was, in a way, willingly unwitting
to a terrible truth?

I ask the same question
of my desperate,
and very likely, futile attempt
to change the outcome.
Perhaps for both, it is both.

Apart

I long for you.

I hunger,

I thirst.

But I have become the desert.

I hold my breath,

hunt for your heartbeat.

Now, even mine is still.

I am stone.

I search for you

and find only shadow,

your warmth a faraway memory.

I am the dark side of the moon.

Discriminating Taste

He's got no style.
High-water department store slacks.
Eight-dollar polo made by eight-year-olds in Bangladesh.
White tube socks, are you kidding?

Complaining every year
how he wasn't promoted, yet again.
Even though his numbers were better
than most everyone else's.

If he's so smart,
why doesn't he dress for the next level?
Because he's socially incompetent
and he's got no style. Right?

She's so fat.
Why is she even at the gym?
She'll be talking fast and wide-eyed
tomorrow at her lunch break.

Way, way too eager.
Her coworkers will pretend
to be interested and listening
about how many miles she "ran" on the treadmill.

And all about how so few people are there at six a.m.,
a dab of mayonnaise on her cheek
as she scarfs down a footlong.
Disgusting, don't you agree?

They're all a bunch of losers.
Every Friday night
they're at the bowling alley
(and not the nice one uptown).

Each one is bent more on swilling skunky beer
than rolling a 300, while back at home
their future ex-wives lap up microwave dinners
washed down with half a box of high-sulfite wine.

Lamentably, their Darwin-defying progeny are routinely made
incrementally dumber by the latest reality TV ignominies
and social media syndromes.
Wash, rinse, repeat.

He's a maven at reading people.

Everyone is sized up in record time.

Clothes, shoes, fitness, looks,

weight, bust size, haircut.

Car, watch, address,

gait, eye contact, mannerisms, smile (or lack thereof).

Vocabulary, accent, emotional control,

confidence, intelligence, sociability.

Ten seconds, plus or minus, is usually all it takes.

They are then tucked away.

Assessed, graded, categorized, filed.

It's a scientific system. Beautiful, in a way. *Don't you think?*

Sideways

In, further in.

Farther, too fast?

Then, stop. Nowhere.

Nothing perfect can last.

Gasping and grasping at air.

Gone for good, all that mattered—

something so real, so right, right there…

Only photos are left. There is nothing else at all.

Mementos of how it is to be right at the edge, and never fall.

Greener

I tell people I am happy.
I tell them all the reasons—I have
challenge, engagement, opportunity, and purpose.

Then comes a knock at the door, all bright and shiny
with fancy words promising
inspiration, influence, intrigue, and joy.

It is difficult not to be distracted
by the next *definitely the best thing ever.*
But things are not always what they seem.

I think I will take my time and feel it out.
Sometimes, the grass is greener.
Sometimes, it is sick.

Salvage

It's all good, trust me.
On the up-and-up.
Hard to believe, yes,
but I've got it, nonetheless.
This is your best option, for sure.

Everything's fine, no need for worry.
Just keep doing what you need to do,
all those five-star, weighty tasks.
I'll take care of these things,
just leave them with me.

Time will pass and you may wonder
if I've kept my promises.
You might be concerned
that it no longer appears
to be on the up-and-up.

You may decide you've completed

your front page

world-changing endeavors,

at least to the point

you should check and...

What's that now?

Yes I remember you.

That was some time ago,

how've you been?

Excuse me? What are you talking about?

No, I think you have it wrong.

I've been here all along.

I remember no promises,

no assurances,

nothing like that.

You left everything with real value behind

and now it's all gone.

Where have you been? This is life, my friend.

You can't just walk away and come back later

claiming this and that.

This is how it works.

Trust me.

I know what I'm talking about.

I've been here

all along.

What was

so important

that you left all this

unattended

in the first place?

Nothing

I wandered into a maelstrom,
unaware of the buffeting wind.
Oblivious to cutting sheets of rain,
the stink of scorched earth and ozone.

Because it was dark,
and because I felt nothing.

Nothing hid my pain,
torment incepted by the loss of everything.
Nothing masked my memory
of her and us, of joy.

Nothing was a gift.
Nothing hurts me now.

Fortune Favors Me

Awakening

Avoid the inelegance
of assumption,
the astigmatism
of disregard.

Free your thoughts.

Want to Want

What is the most positive
and rewarding thing in life?
I believe it is to concern oneself more
with the needs of others.

But it must be done for them.
Not to make oneself feel good, or better.
It must be genuine and unconditional.
You must want to do it *just for them*.

I have been the worst at this
for so long,
and I am still continually challenged
in following my own advice.

I fail often, and sometimes, badly.
How do I learn to want something, really want it,
when it may have no apparent benefit for me?
When it may be difficult?

As is the case with all things worthwhile,

it takes dedication and practice.

Making it easier along the way

is *wanting to want it.*

Ephemeris

Forego the fantasy
of wishing on a star.

Instead, use it to navigate
to a better place.

Thanks

Awoken so rudely, alarming thoughts.
I will have to do more with less.
Miles behind milestones, connecting the dots,
my job is a challenging mess.

The house, a tornadic experiment
for kids with (I'm sure) ADD.
I've yet to get up, already I'm spent.
OK, here we go *one two three*…

Glare at the mirror while trying to smile
to spite all the lines on my face.
Perhaps if I shake my head for a while
good thoughts may just fall into place.

Notwithstanding all the anxiety,
I try to reflect on the good.
My life is of the variety
most people would have if they could.

Thank God I'm not sick or immobilized
My health is not bad, and I'm fit.
Though work leaves me fit to be traumatized,
the income, it helps quite a bit.

Providing nourishment, clothing and home,
tornadic as all that may be,
and sustained by a family maelstrom
I love more than life, more than me…

Visage now changed in a positive way,
awakened, on this I concede.
I turn from the mirror, welcome the day
with thanks—this is all that I need.

Ad Astra per Aspera

A goal without a plan,
without strategy and execution,
is nothing other than a wish.
A goal without a backup plan
is but a wager.

Chart your approach, callous your hands.
Never wish for anything.
Mitigate and eliminate uncertainty.
Study the stars, watch the weather,
trim your sails.

Winning

Success

driven by an insatiable compulsion

to triumph at all costs

is a byproduct of narcissism.

Rotten fruit.

Strive each day to do your best in all things.

Help others do the same.

You will begin to care less about conquering

and more about winning.

Vector

It is not enough to be driven—
to have passion,
energy, resilience, grit.

Without purpose or direction,
to be driven
is simply fuel for false hope.

Beware becoming the inadvertent passenger
hurtling eagerly along a road to nowhere.
Drive.

Further

I was wanting, waiting on an unlikely dream.

As if stirred to life from fantasy,

it beckoned as it came for me.

An arousing adventure with risk, real as rain.

I waded in, the water warm and deep.

Headlong and boldly then, I dove.

He must be mad, some said,

while others saw it as providence.

I suspect it to be some combination thereof.

If I am right, it should not matter of course

that I could be crazy because as luck would have it,

fortune favors me.

I Am

Qui Verra Vivra

The way we think—
how we see things,
what we decide to believe,

and those we share our journey with
greatly influence
the path we choose and how we follow it.

Continually challenging the legitimacy of our thoughts
and surrounding ourselves with those who do likewise
makes it simpler to understand what is true, and what is not.

We can then rest easy with the realization
we are moving in the right direction,
which enables us to live life to its fullest.

The Reality of Us

Early bird or strike while it's hot—
pick your cliché.
I just knew I had to catch your eye
because you wouldn't last a day.

You wore a Penelope Cruz Vanilla Sky jacket from Paris.
Everything about you made my heart smile.
I could sense that January day,
it was as much magical as meant to be.

Coffee and a long conversation.
Not about you or me,
but instead about spirit, change,
life, and joy.

I hugged you goodbye
as you angled in awkwardly for a kiss.
Cute and memorable; perfect, really.
And we laughed.

You changed your plans to meet me,
rendez-vous chez Mon Chou Chou...
We kissed later in an empty courtyard
under a star filled sky lit below by gold glow lamps.

Hearts aflutter, dopey grins, heads buzzing, faces radiating.
Winter days made warm by innumerable
near-surreal synchronicities...
The possibility of us became plausible and then, inevitable.

We both sensed everything was all so simply, *yes*.
To eat together, meditate and play,
travel and adventure together, to love.
All the things.

Our energy was palpable and pure—tuned to the Universe.
Lesser cares melted away into the ether,
replaced each day, more and more,
by the sublime reality of us.

Mindfulness

In the face of distress,
optimism can seem a bridge too far.
By giving our full attention
to the present
and understanding our thoughts and feelings
in the here and now,
the road ahead becomes clearer.

Drive

White knuckling the steering wheel.
Heart pounding, rapt anticipation.
Staring, hard, straight ahead.
Miss you want you wish you were here.

One foot on the brake, one on the gas,
chassis straining, adrenaline rush.
One thing on my mind.
Need you want you make you appear.

Three, two, one,
wanton reckless abandon,
green light, go.
Love you sex you go for a ride.

Upshift upshift upshift, redline.
Zero to ninety, three seconds flat,
full throttle hot motor roaring, losing traction.
Tear through corkscrew brace and collide.

The Reality of Verity

You will never be more honest
than when you are praying.
No matter who you believe God to be.
After all,
what is the point in lying to God?

You will never even color the truth,
use intonation
to shape perception,
adjust body language
to influence an outcome.

You will never attempt to
choose
your
words
carefully.

When you pray,

your honesty is

perfect.

Prayer is rehearsal of

truth.

Without truth, no one will ever understand

who you really are.

If you are not truly known,

you do not exist in the true sense of the word.

You cannot be.

Without truth,

you

are

counterfeit,

a shadow.

You

I saw a picture of you
that told me you were kind.
Someone beautiful, full of life, refined.

As if in a dream, I imagined you as real,
wanting more of how your photo made me feel.
I asked to meet you, and you said to me, *why not?*

Then waiting, held captive, caught
by the impossible image of a girl who never arrived.
Instead, you walked through the door.
And you were so, so much more.

Faith

I cannot see or hear it but was told it is there.
No one has showed me where to find it.
A metaphysical concept, wholly unfair,
that tells me without it, I'm blinded.

That without it I am lost, with no true direction
and will never really find my way.
That if I am seeking some level of perfection
I must trust it exists, every day.

That with it, I will be able to follow a path
with purpose and a confident stride
to gracefully meet life in the face of its wrath,
and with like-minded friends at my side.

Serenity

Fear

is oftentimes borne

of ignorance and misconception.

It lays waste

to the landscape of the soul.

Continually strive for knowledge

and improvement of self.

What follows is a deeper, more accurate,

and comforting conception of the world,

and of your most befitting place within.

Am I?

Ah, empathy.
How painfully difficult to master.
To comprehend how others feel.
To be capable of relating,
not to what they say or do, rather,
to their associated thoughts.

I think, therefore I am.
They think, then they must be.
Yet they do not think as I. Not remotely.
And in my careful assessment,
I feel they think wrongly.
That they then may not exist as do I.

Ergo, I am, and *they are not quite*. Potentially lesser.
So, do I exist alone? An unappealing predicament.
And the alternative, more iniquitous,
is that *my* thoughts are spurious.
That *they are*, and *I am not quite*.
That I am the lesser and I do not exist as do they.

What if I accept there may be an aberration in how I think?
What if I try to acknowledge and assess the impairment,
and then to better understand the thinking of others?
I believe both must be done for either to be done.
I can then perform a translation of sorts,
which allows me to see myself and others *as we are*.

This does not mean their thinking is right.
However, I am now awakened to how they might be wrong.
If I can empathize with others, genuinely connect
my thoughts and experiences with theirs,
I will never be challenged in affirming that
I am.

I Know Why
We Are Here

Title

I did not know you existed.

That it was possible.

The concept of you

was beyond me.

Even now,

I am still amazed.

I think of you,

shake my head, and smile.

You make me feel…

the way I feel.

And I simply do not

have the words.

Spirituality

It is not

a complex thing.

It is also something

that is not easily mastered.

We must be dedicated

to continuous improvement

and knowledge of self

and then, work to achieve

a deeper understanding

of those around us,

of our environment, and

of our place in it.

It is

a normalized state

of persistent self-awareness and personal growth

achieved in harmony with others.

Everything

I feel all of you.

My lips to yours, just touching.

I trace the tip of my tongue

along the hollow of your neck.

Your skin against mine,

you pull me in.

Pressing me to you,

holding me there.

I sense your heartbeat quicken,

matching our rhythm.

Your breath on my chest as you say my name,

a vulnerable whisper.

I stare into your eyes, your soul,

and know the visceral depth of your passion,

burning and growing as it joins with mine,

feeding mine, mine feeding yours.

I feel you.

So acutely, so completely.

All of you, everything,

all at once.

Friend

I am full with gratitude,
you are my dearest friend.
When I was down on luck and life,
you stayed right through the end.

Patient, caring, showing me
how empathy revives
love and positivity,
and spirit in our lives.

My thoughts are with you always,
together or apart.
Thank you, friend, I love you
from the bottom my heart.

When

When I grow and can *feel it*,
and know I am
becoming a better person.

When I see the things I do
sow seeds of goodness in others.

When life is quick and bold
and multilayered,
and I know it will soon pass.

When I realize how lucky I am,
in the moment, to savor it all…

— *Hannah Zenn*

Love

Your smile
elevates me,
warms my heart,
validates my existence.

Sandstorm

From this distance,

it almost does not move.

Impressive in size—majestic,

even more so against the backdrop

of an expansive, jagged valley mountain horizon.

Despite its grandeur and apparent power, all is calm.

Were it not for our eyes, the storm would not exist.

But it so obviously does and as we approach, it changes.

It is now impossible to tell if we have yet to enter

or are already inside...

Its edges are indiscernible.

We see instead a medium of light, billowing hazes,

transparent and wispy

and gaining substance further in

until our path ahead is largely obscured.

Superfine yellow-white dust swirls along the road.

A vast carpet of interconnected pinwheel patterns

floating from right to left in front of us,

jumping over and around rocks and desert debris.

Everything still supranaturally silent.

We slow to a stop and observe.

There is no one else, no one near, just us.

Mesmerized, I wonder if you feel as I do.

I glance over, and in your own remarkable way,

you seem to find our otherworldly experience whimsical.

Your abrupt, carefree laughter

enlivens the magic of the moment,

surreal to real.

In an instant,

I know why we are here.

Φ

About The Author

JOHN CASEY is Pushcart Prize-nominated poet and novelist from New Hampshire. He is the author of *Raw Thoughts: A Mindful Fusion of Poetic and Photographic Art*, *Meridian: A Raw Thoughts Book*, and *The Devolution Trilogy*, a psychological spy thriller series. A Veteran combat and test pilot, Casey also served as a diplomat and international affairs strategist at U.S. embassies in Europe and Africa, the Pentagon, and elsewhere. He is passionate about fitness, nature, and the human spirit and inspired by the incredible spectrum of people, places, and cultures he has experienced in life.

Visit

https://johnjcasey.com

for more on his books and writing.